Contents

Welcome to Space

You have an amazing job – you're an astronaut! You will be taking your first trip into space very soon. What will it be like? You think it will be fun to be weightless and float around your rocket. You're also looking forward to seeing planet Earth out of the window. Let's go!

Lots of people want to be astronauts.
The people who are chosen have some special skills.

Astronauts are scientists and carry out important research.

Some astronauts are top pilots. They fly rockets and planes.

Anyone who goes into space must be very fit.

You're living in a tiny space, so you must get on well with other people.

But did you know that astronauts have to use maths?

USING MATHS

JOURNEY TO THE MOON

Wendy Clemson and David Clemson

ticktock

Copyright © ticktock Entertainment Ltd 2007
First published in Great Britain in 2007 by ticktock Media Ltd.,
Unit 2, Orchard Business Centre, North Farm Road,
Tunbridge Wells, Kent, TN2 3XF

ticktock project editor: Rebecca Clunes
ticktock project designer: Sara Greasley

ISBN 978 1 84696 059 8

Printed in China

Picture credits
t=top, b=bottom, c=centre, l-left, r=right, f=far
Christian Deforeit 15; **ESA/J Huart** 3FL, 6L; **NASA** 5, 8, 10, 16B, 16T, 17T, 22, 23, 24B, 24T, 25, 26, 29T, 29B;
Jerry Mason/Science Photo Library 19; **Science Photo Library/NASA** 17B, 27;
Detlev van Ravenswaay/Science Photo Library 20-21B; **Shutterstock** 1, 4 (all), 9B, 11, 12-13 (all), 31T, 31B;
Ticktock Media archive 2, 3L, 3C, 3R, 3FR, 6-7, 9T, 20, 21TL, 21TR, 28, 30.
Cover images: all from Ticktock Media Archive except front cover main pictureof astronaut from NASA.

Every effort has been made to trace the copyright holders, and we apologise in advance for any unintentional omissions.
We would be pleased to insert the appropriate acknowledgements in any subsequent edition of this publication.

In this book you will find lots of number puzzles that astronauts have to solve every day. You will also get the chance to answer lots of number questions about your space adventure.

What's inside the book?

Find out what it's like to be an astronaut.

Answer the questions and practise your maths skills.

If you get stuck, there are some tips to help you on pages 30-31.

The charts and tables will help you answer the maths questions.

Look out for facts about space.

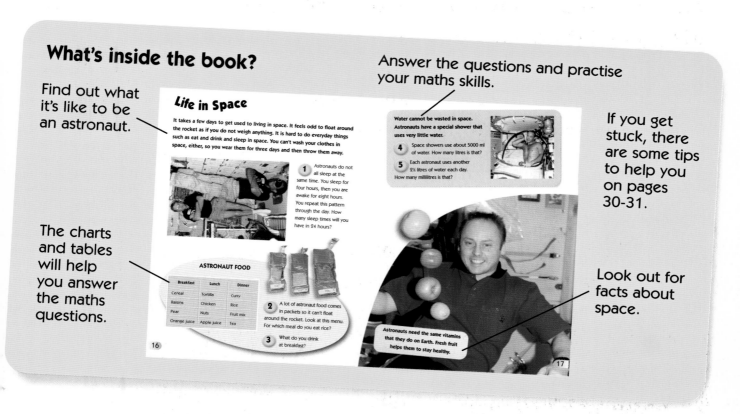

Life in Space

It takes a few days to get used to living in space. It feels odd to float around the rocket as if you do not weigh anything. It is hard to do everyday things such as eat and drink and sleep in space. You can't wash your clothes in space, either, so you wear them for three days and then throw them away.

1 Astronauts do not all sleep at the same time. You sleep for four hours, then you are awake for eight hours. You repeat this pattern through the day. How many sleep times will you have in 24 hours?

ASTRONAUT FOOD

Breakfast	Lunch	Dinner
Cereal	Tortilla	Curry
Raisins	Chicken	Rice
Pear	Nuts	Fruit mix
Orange juice	Apple juice	Tea

2 A lot of astronaut food comes in packets so it can't float around the rocket. Look at this menu. For which meal do you eat rice?

3 What do you drink at breakfast?

Water cannot be wasted in space. Astronauts have a special shower that uses very little water.

4 Space showers use about 5000 ml of water. How many litres is that?

5 Each astronaut uses another 2½ litres of water each day. How many millilitres is that?

Astronauts need the same vitamins that they do on Earth. Fresh fruit helps them to stay healthy.

16

17

Are you ready to be an astronaut?

You will need paper and pencil, and don't forget your space suit! Let's go...

Heading for the Moon

You have been chosen to take part in a mission to the Moon. Your space rocket will blast off into space and travel 384,400 kilometres to the Moon. Your mission will take about a week. Let's find out about the Moon!

Have you noticed the Moon's changing shape? It takes 29 days from one full Moon to the next. This is called a lunar month.

1 How many days are there in 2 lunar months?

2 Is 29 an odd number or an even number?

THE SHAPE OF THE MOON

The Moon seems to change its shape during the lunar month. Here are some of the shapes we can see.

A   B   C   D   E

3 Which of these shapes is a circle?

4 What is the shape of Moon C?

Earth

Moon

The Moon is about 4 times smaller than the Earth.

A journey to the Moon is as far as driving around the Earth about ten times! See if you can answer these questions about x10.

5 Every day you run 3 kilometres. How many miles would you go if you ran 10 times as far?

6 You love to drink milk. You have 200 ml. How much would you have if you drank 10 times this amount?

7 Your have a pet mouse. Imagine if she were 10 times as long! Would she be the size of:

A a guinea pig   B a dog   C an elephant

Astronaut Training

It takes a long time to learn how to be an astronaut. Your training is hard but fun. You learn how to fly the rocket, how to breathe in your space suit and how to walk in space. You make friends with the other people training to be astronauts.

ASTRONAUT CHART

Name	Tim	Cilla	Leo
Age	19 years	22 years	25 years
Height	180 cm	150 cm	200 cm

1 You start training with Tim, Cilla and Leo. It will be ten years before you all go into space. How old will these astronauts be when you go into space?

2 The first rockets ever made were very small. Only short people fitted into them. Which of these astronauts would fit best into a small rocket?

3 Astronauts wear a special suit in space. Space suits weigh around 22 kg. 22 comes between 20 and 30. What other whole numbers come between 20 and 30?

FLIGHT TRAINING

As part of your training you have to learn how to fly a jet. It is important for you to be able to steer the plane.

4 The fighter plane below has made a ¼ turn clockwise. Which other planes have made a ¼ turn?

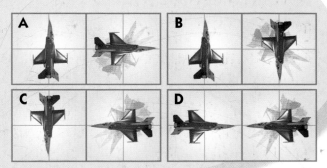

There is no air in space. When astronauts go outside the rocket, they wear a space suit, which gives them oxygen to breathe.

The Space Rocket

You have finished your training and you're ready to go to the Moon. The space rocket is ready too! You go to look at it. It's hard to believe that this will be your home for the next week.

The bottom of the rocket looks like this. It has five pipes. They have been arranged in a pattern like this.

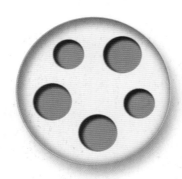

1 Which of these rockets has its pipes arranged in the same way?

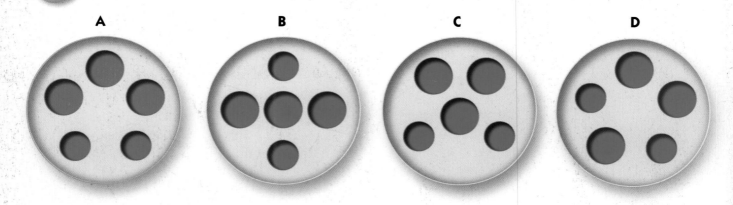

A   B   C   D

2 The rocket can sit on the launch pad for several weeks. This clock shows how many hours, minutes and seconds there are until its launch. Is this

about a week?   about 1 day?

about 2 days?   about ½ day?

Can you find this shape on the tower?

3 How many sides are on this shape?

4 How many corners does this shape have?

The engines are at the bottom of the rocket. The astronauts sit near the top of the rocket.

5 We can find these shapes in the rocket. Can you name them?

Your rocket is ready to blast off into space!

We Have Lift Off!

This is it! You say goodbye to your family and friends and climb into the space rocket. You do the final checks and then strap yourself into your seat. The rocket starts to shake. Boom! You have lift off!

At 10 am the fuel is loaded into the space rocket. 3 hours later you get into the space rocket. It then takes you 2 hours to do the final checks. 1 hour after that, the rocket launches into space!

1 Can you work out what time the rocket will be launched?

2 Astronauts have to be good at counting forwards and back. Can you work out the missing numbers in these counting patterns?

A   3   6   ?   12

B   25   30   35   ?

C   22   ?   18   16

After lift off, parts of the rocket fall away.
This makes the rocket lighter, so it can go faster.
This line shows when each part falls off.

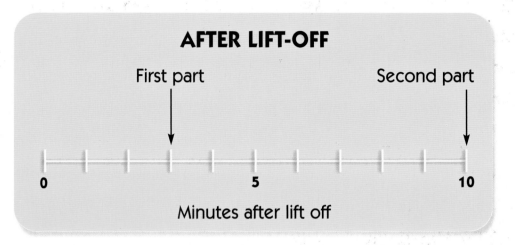

AFTER LIFT-OFF

First part   Second part

0   5   10

Minutes after lift off

3 How many minutes after lift off does the first part fall away?

4 How many minutes after lift off does the second part fall away?

Missions to the Moon have three astronauts, but only two of them get to walk on the Moon. For safety reasons, one person has to stay in the rocket.

The Stars In Space

Your space rocket has a window, and whenever you can, you look out at the stars. Wow! There are so many of them. They seem much brighter in space. A pattern of stars is called a constellation. There are 88 constellations in the sky around you.

Here is a constellation number track.

77		79	80						87	88

1 Which of these numbers would NOT go into this number track?

71   85   76   89   86   84

2 This group of stars is called the Plough. How many stars can you see in this constellation?

3 How many lines are there between the stars in the Plough?

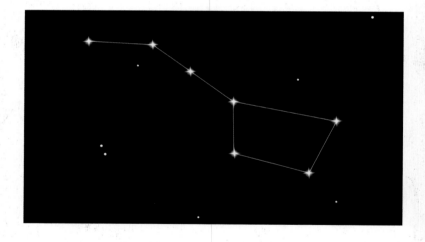

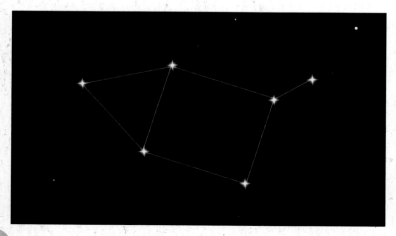

4 You see a new constellation. How many stars make the triangle?

5 How many stars make the rectangle?

14

There are 7 types of stars. One of the biggest is the red supergiant. It is much bigger than our Sun. A white dwarf is one of the smallest stars. You will have to count stars on your trip. Try this star maths.

6 11 red supergiants
plus 8 red supergiants

7 14 red supergiants
take away 13 red supergiants

8 9 white dwarfs added to
17 white dwarfs

9 30 white dwarfs minus
22 white dwarfs

We can see the stars much better from space. The Earth's atmosphere makes it hard to see the night sky clearly.

Life in Space

It takes a few days to get used to living in space. It feels odd to float around the rocket as if you do not weigh anything. It is hard to do everyday things such as eat and drink and sleep in space. You can't wash your clothes in space, either, so you wear them for three days and then throw them away.

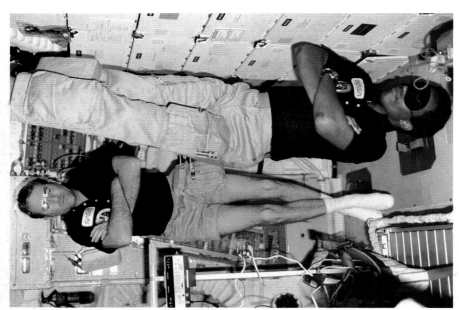

1 Astronauts do not all sleep at the same time. You sleep for four hours, then you are awake for eight hours. You repeat this pattern through the day. How many sleep times will you have in 24 hours?

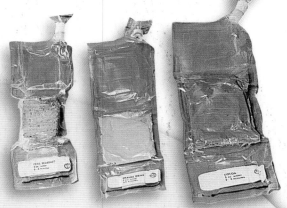

ASTRONAUT FOOD

Breakfast	Lunch	Dinner
Cereal	Tortilla	Curry
Raisins	Chicken	Rice
Pear	Nuts	Fruit mix
Orange juice	Apple juice	Tea

2 A lot of astronaut food comes in packets so it can't float around the rocket. Look at this menu. For which meal do you eat rice?

3 What do you drink at breakfast?

16

Water cannot be wasted in space. Astronauts have a special shower that uses very little water.

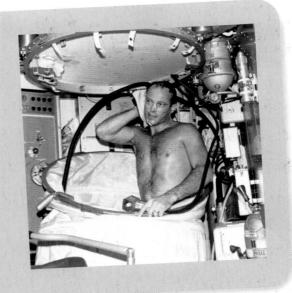

4 Space showers use about 5000 ml of water. How many litres is that?

5 Each astronaut uses another 2½ litres of water each day. How many millilitres is that?

Astronauts need the same vitamins that they do on Earth. Fresh fruit helps them to stay healthy.

Back at Mission Control

Back on Earth, there are lots of people in the mission control room. They check that the space rocket is working properly and the astronauts are healthy. They use computers linked to the rocket to get their data.

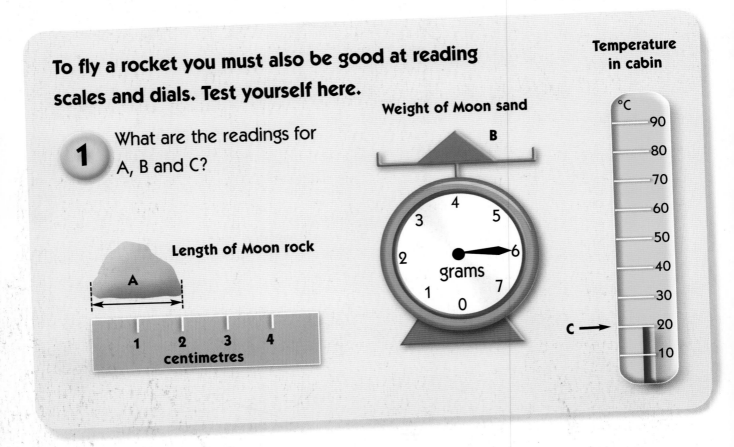

To fly a rocket you must also be good at reading scales and dials. Test yourself here.

1 What are the readings for A, B and C?

Weight of Moon sand

Length of Moon rock

Temperature in cabin

There are red and green lights on the computers. The green means everything is working, the red means something is wrong. Look at this pattern of lights.

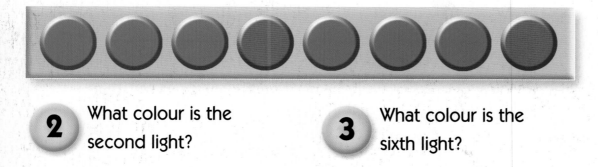

2 What colour is the second light?

3 What colour is the sixth light?

In space, you and the rest of the crew feel weightless. You can float around the rocket.

This food bar feels weightless, too. On Earth it weighs 20 grams.

4 How much do these bars weigh on Earth?

5 How much do these bars weigh on Earth?

6 Mission control needs to check that you're not too tired and your brain is working. Here is a thinking puzzle for you. What is the mystery number?

| A mystery number | − | 4 | = | 8 |

Mission control can send commands to the space rocket's computers, even though they are thousands of kilometres apart.

Our Solar System

If your journey to the Moon goes well, you might be picked to take part in a mission to the planet Mars. Our Solar System has eight planets. Earth is one of them. Astronauts need to know about the other planets.

Look at the picture at the bottom of this page.
It shows all of the planets in our Solar System.

1 Which planets are nearer to the Sun than Earth?

2 Is Mars bigger than Earth?

3 Which is bigger – Earth or Neptune?

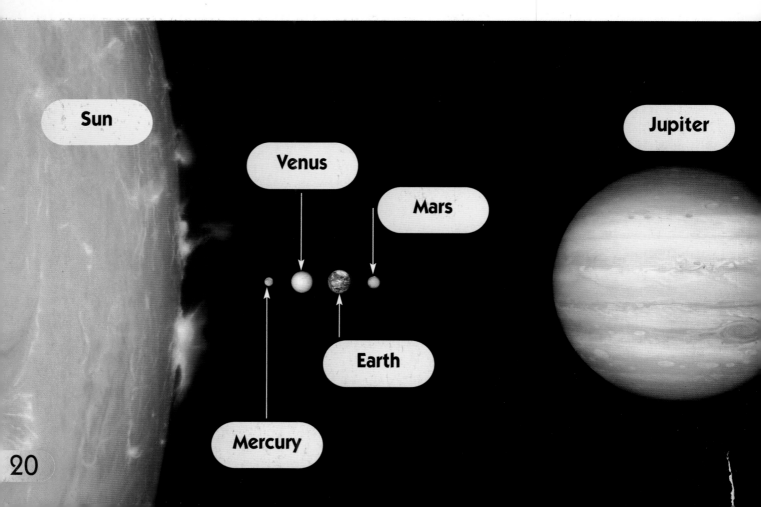

Sun

Venus

Mars

Jupiter

Earth

Mercury

The planets closest to Earth are Venus and Mars.

4 Which of these planets is called the Red Planet?

5 Which of these planets has two moons?

VENUS FACTS
- It is very hot.
- Covered in gases.
- It doesn't have any moons.

MARS FACTS
- It is cold.
- It is called the Red Planet.
- It has 2 moons.

6 Earth only has one moon. Neptune, Jupiter and Uranus have lots of moons. One of these planets has 15 moons, one has 8 moons and one has 16 moons.
- Jupiter has the most moons.
- Neptune has the fewest moons.

Can you say how many moons Neptune, Jupiter and Uranus have?

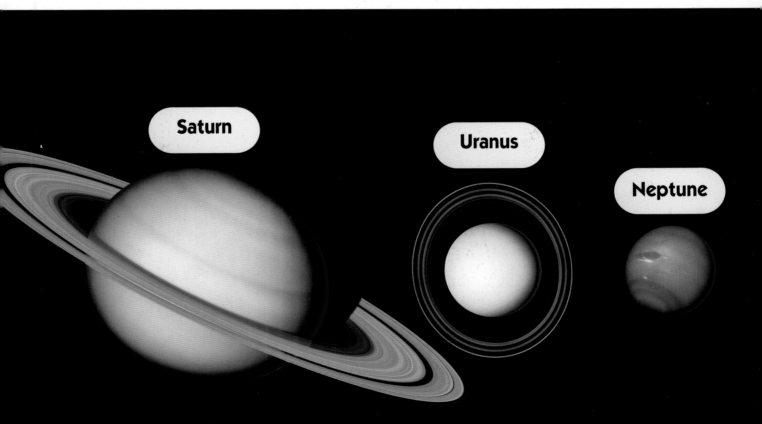

Saturn

Uranus

Neptune

Landing on the Moon

Your rocket is near the Moon. The Moon Lander part of the rocket breaks off and takes you to the Moon's surface. You look out of the window. The Moon has rocky mountains and big holes called craters. It is dry and dusty. You and the other astronauts are the only living things on the Moon.

There are big holes, or craters, on the Moon. The craters are made when rocks from space crash into the Moon. Your task is to measure some crater widths. Here are your results:

**10 cm   ½ metre   9 metres
90 cm   2 m**

1 Put the measurements in order, starting with the shortest width.

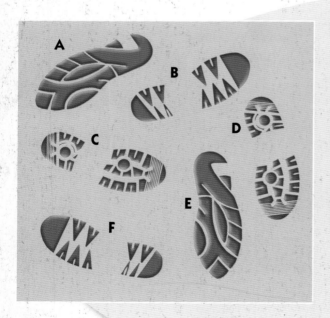

There is no wind on the Moon. You look out of the window and see footprints left behind by other astronauts. Your footprints will also be there long after you leave.

2 Match up the pairs of astronaut footprints.

3 How many astronauts have made these footprints?

You won't be the first astronaut on the Moon. The first men to ever walk the Moon were from the Apollo II, in 1969. Here is their mission calendar:

July 1969					
Sunday		7	14	21	28
Monday	1	8	15	22	29
Tuesday	2	9	16	23	30
Wednesday	3	10	17	24	31
Thursday	4	11	18	25	
Friday	5	12	19	26	
Saturday	6	13	20	27	

16th July - Blast off!

20th July - Landing on the Moon

21st July - First person steps on the Moon

21st July - Lift off!

24th July - Arrive back on Earth

4 On which day of the week did the the first person step on the Moon?

5 Did the mission take over a week or under a week?

This is it! You're about to step on to the Moon!

Walking On the Moon

The door to your Moon Lander opens slowly. You walk down the steps and then step on to the Moon. This is it! You are actually here! Walking on the Moon is fun. You weigh much less here than you do on Earth, so walking is more like bouncing.

FINDING YOUR WAY

You have a grid map of part of the Moon.

Moon Lander   **crater**   **small rock**   **large rock**

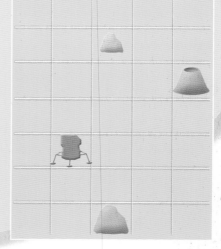

1 The small rock is 1 square right and 3 squares up from the Moon Lander. What are the directions from the Moon Lander to reach the crater?

2 How would you reach the large rock from the Moon Lander?

3 You have been asked to collect some rocks from the Moon. Back on Earth, scientists will study them to find out more about the Moon. You collect 20 kilograms of Moon rock. How many boxes will you need if each box can carry 4 kilograms of Moon rock?

4 How many boxes will you need if each box can carry 5 kilograms?

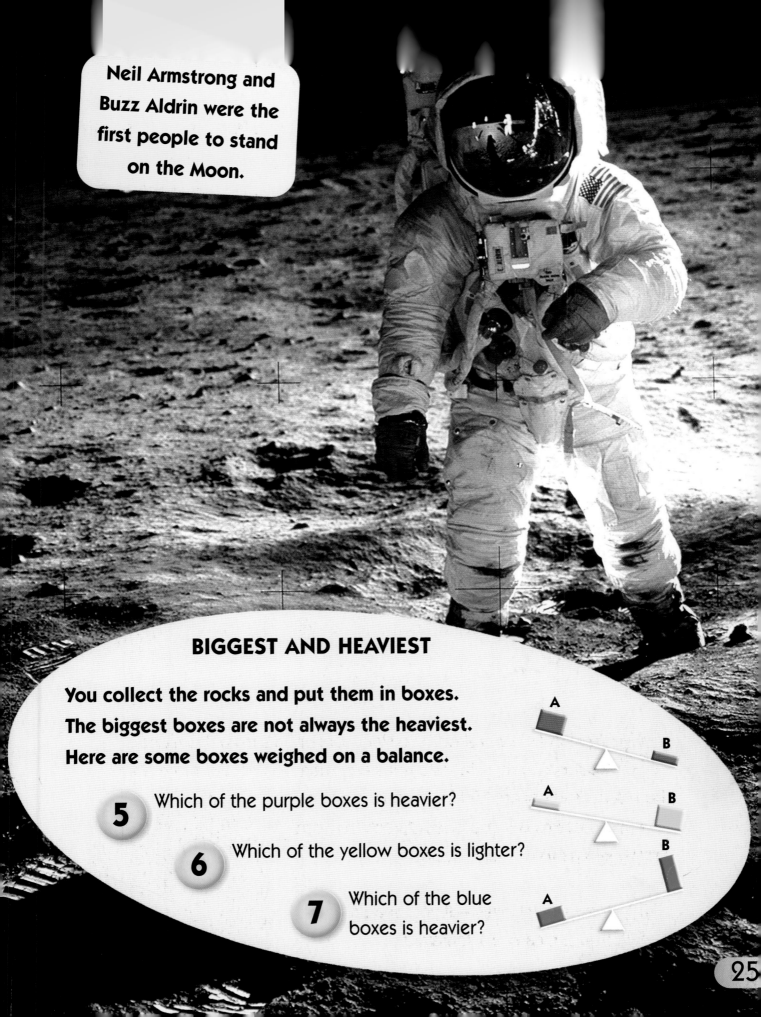

Neil Armstrong and Buzz Aldrin were the first people to stand on the Moon.

BIGGEST AND HEAVIEST

You collect the rocks and put them in boxes. The biggest boxes are not always the heaviest. Here are some boxes weighed on a balance.

5 Which of the purple boxes is heavier?

6 Which of the yellow boxes is lighter?

7 Which of the blue boxes is heavier?

Return to Earth

The rocket is carrying a capsule. When you get near Earth you all get into the capsule. The capsule comes away from the rocket and brings you back to Earth. You splash down safely into the sea. Your mission has been a success.

The capsule goes very fast.

1 Can you put these in order of how fast they are? Start with the fastest.

running cheetah – 100 kilometres per hour

capsule – 38 000 kilometres per hour

fastest train – 400 kilometres per hour

2 The capsule has three parachutes to slow it down. One parachute has 20 strings. What do we need to add to these numbers to make 20?

19   7   3   16

SPLASH DOWN IN THE SEA

You come down into the sea. There are lots of people around, on planes, ships and helicopters.

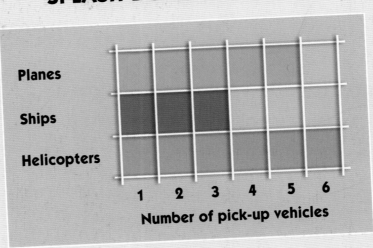

Planes

Ships

Helicopters

1   2   3   4   5   6

Number of pick-up vehicles

3 How many helicopters are there?

4 How many vehicles are there in total?

Your capsule splashes into the water. You've made a safe landing.

YOU'RE HOME!

Your capsule lands in the sea at 2:00 pm. Here are the times that you and the other astronauts actually step out of the capsule.

Leo	2:11 pm
Cilla	2:06 pm
You	2:13 pm
Tim	2:09 pm

5 Who is first out of the capsule?

6 How many minutes after landing are all the space team out?

Back Home

You have landed safely back on Earth. It's been an amazing trip. Of course, everybody wants to hear about it. Reporters from newspapers and TV crowd around you, wanting to hear your story. You are famous!

Here's what happens after your capsule crashes into the sea. First, you need to find out the answer to the number puzzle. Then, you can answer the question.

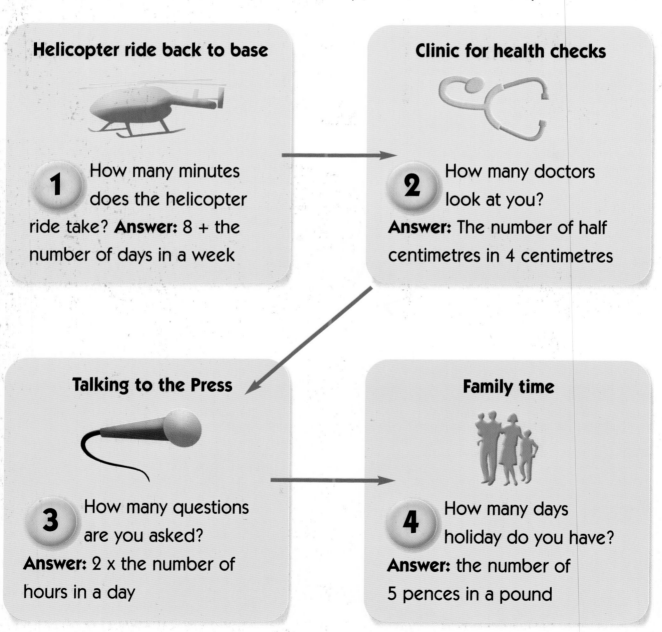

Helicopter ride back to base

1 How many minutes does the helicopter ride take? **Answer:** 8 + the number of days in a week

Clinic for health checks

2 How many doctors look at you? **Answer:** The number of half centimetres in 4 centimetres

Talking to the Press

3 How many questions are you asked? **Answer:** 2 x the number of hours in a day

Family time

4 How many days holiday do you have? **Answer:** the number of 5 pences in a pound

5 Each space mission has a badge. This is the Apollo 11 badge. Look at the three badges below.
Which badge did your mission choose?

- It has two circles to show Earth and the Moon.
- It has a triangle to represent the space rocket.
- It has a square to represent the 4 astronauts on your team. Which is your badge?

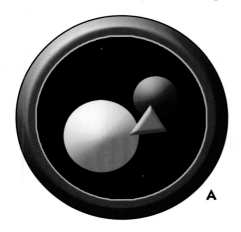 **A**

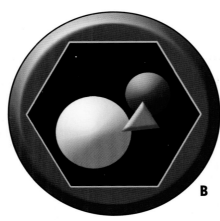 **B**

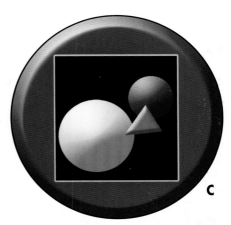 **C**

The next team of astronauts is ready to go up into space, but your mission is over now. Well done, astronaut!

Tips and Help

PAGES 6-7

Odds and evens – Even numbers are in the pattern of counting in twos: 2 4 6 8 and so on. Odd numbers are those that are not even: 1 3 5 7 and so on.

PAGES 8-9

Adding ten – When you add ten to a number you need only increase the tens in that number by 1 ten; so 19 has one ten (and nine ones) and if we add a ten to make two tens the answer is 29 (two tens and nine ones).

A ¼ turn – There are four quarter turns in one complete turn

Clockwise – Clockwise is the direction the hands of a clock move around.

clockwise

PAGES 10-11

Number of hours in a day – There are 12 hours in half a day, 24 hours in one day, 48 hours in two days, and 168 hours in a week.

Shapes – Remember these shapes:

Cylinder: the two faces at the ends of a cylinder are circles

Cone: a cone has a flat circular base.

PAGES 12-13

Telling the time – The shorter hand on a clock is the hour hand (It tells us what o'clock). Move the hour hand on 3 hours, then 2 hours, and then 1 hour and you have launch time.

Number line – The number line here is measuring minutes. Each mark on the line means one minute.

PAGES 14-15

Adding up – The words plus, add up, add to and sum all mean the same. You can add numbers in any order. As it can be easier to add 10, if you find 11 or 9 in a sum, you could add 10 and then take away or add 1 to the answer.

11 + 8 gives the same answer as 10 + 8 + 1
9 + 17 gives the same answer as 10 + 17 − 1

Taking away – Take away, minus and subtract all mean the same.

PAGES 16-17

Day – There are 24 hours in a day; that is from midnight to the next midnight.

PAGES 18-19

Scales and dials – In maths these help us 'read off' measures. Check which measure is shown. For example this scale shows us grams.

Counting in twos – Count aloud: 2 4 6 8 10 12 14 16 18 20. It is useful to remember this pattern.

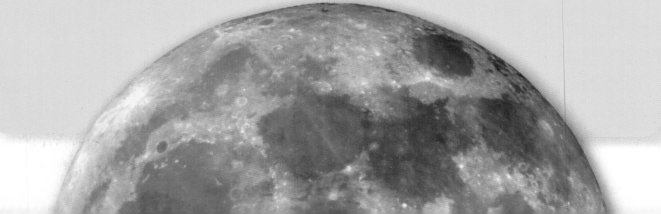

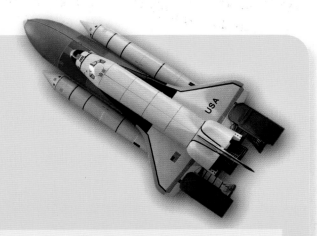

PAGES 20-21

Comparing things – We say bigger than when we compare two things, and biggest when we compare three or more than three things. We say 'more', or 'fewer' when we compare two numbers and 'most' or 'fewest' when we compare three or more than three numbers.

PAGES 22-23

Putting measures in order – Check that all the measurements are in the same unit (that is, are they all centimetres or metres?) If not, change them all to the same units. Next, put the numbers in order. The smallest whole numbers have no tens (only ones or units). They are the numbers 1 2 3 4 5 6 7 8 9. Next, look for numbers with only 1 ten and put the number with fewest units first, then the others. Then see if there are numbers with more than 1 ten and put those in order of the number of tens they have and so on.

Calendar – A calendar tells us the day of the week for each date in a month. We can 'read' a calendar down or across. On this calendar, 'reading' down gives us the dates for a week, across tells us the dates for each day (for example, all the Sundays).

PAGES 24-25

Grid maps – You can work out the routes on a grid map by moving right or left and up or down (or up or down and then right or left).

Sharing – When we break up an amount or a number into equal parts each part is a share or fraction of the whole. This is called sharing or dividing.

PAGES 26-27

Making 20 – It is useful to know the pairs of numbers that sum to 20. See if you can continue the pattern:
0 + 20
1 + 19
2 + 18......

Block graph – This chart compares two kinds of information. In this block graph one 'block' means one pick-up vehicle and the graph compares numbers of kinds of vehicle.

Digital time – We can tell digital time by 'reading off' the hours and then the minutes. For example, 8:27 am means the time is 27 minutes past 8 in the morning.

PAGES 28-29

Measures – Remember there are:
- 7 days in a week
- 2 halves in a whole one
- 100 pence in a pound.

Answers

PAGES 6-7

1. 58
2. odd
3. E
4. semi-circle
5. 30 kilometres
6. 2000 ml or 2 litres
7. a dog

PAGES 8-9

1. Tim – 29 years old
   Cilla – 32 years old
   Leo – 35 years old
2. Cilla
3. 21, 23, 24, 25, 26, 27, 28 and 29
4. A and C

PAGES 10-11

1. D
2. about 1 day
3. 4
4. 4
5. cylinder and cone

PAGES 12-13

1. 4 pm
2. A is 9, B is 40 and C is 20
3. 3 minutes
4. 10 minutes

PAGES 14-15

1. 71, 76 and 89
2. 7
3. 7
4. 3
5. 4
6. 19 red supergiants
7. 1 red supergiant
8. 26 white dwarfs
9. 8 white dwarfs

PAGES 16-17

1. 2 sleep times
2. dinner
3. orange juice
4. 5 litres
5. 2,500 millilitres

PAGES 18-19

1. A is 2 centimetres
   B is 6 grams and
   C is 20°C
2. green
3. green
4. 40 grams
5. 100 grams
6. 12

PAGES 20-21

1. Mercury and Venus
2. no
3. Neptune
4. Mars
5. Mars
6. Jupiter has 16 moons, Uranus has 15 moons, and Neptune has 8 moons

PAGES 22-23

1. 10 cm, ½ metre, 90 cm, 2 m, 9 metres
2. A and E, B and F, C and D
3. 3 astronauts
4. Sunday
5. Over a week

PAGES 24-25

1. 3 squares right and 2 squares up
2. 1 square right, 2 squares down
3. 5 boxes
4. 4 boxes
5. B
6. A
7. A

PAGES 26-27

1. capsule, fastest train, running cheetah
2. 1, 13, 17 and 4
3. 6 helicopters
4. 14 vehicles
5. Cilla
6. 13 minutes

PAGES 28-29

1. 15 minutes
2. 8 doctors
3. 48 questions
4. 20 days
5. C